This BUG Catching Journal Belongs To:

DEDICATION

This Bug Journal is dedicated to all the Bug Finding Lovers out there who love to plan out their bug catching activities, and document their findings in the process.

You are my inspiration for producing books and I'm honored to be a part of keeping all of your bug catching information and records organized.

How to use this Bug Log Book:

This useful bug catching journal is a must-have for anyone that loves to record bug finding activities! You will love this easy to use bug log book to track and record all your bug finding activities.

Each interior page includes space to record & track the following:

Date - Record the date and time of your bug catching adventure.
Season - Checkmark Spring, Summer, Fall or Winter.
Weather Conditions - Use this space to checkmark if it's hot, warm, sunny and so forth.
Bug Name - Stay on task, have the kids do some research to find the type of bug found, and it's name.
Where Did You Find The Bug? - Fill in the location of the found bug.
Number Of Legs - Record the number of legs on the bug.
Bug Description - Checkmark big, shiny, fast, little, and much more.
Photo/Drawing Page - Use this doodle page to sketch out a drawing of the bug, or snap a picture of the bug.
If you are new to collecting bugs or have been at it for a while, this bug finding journal is a must have! Can make a great useful gift for anyone that loves to catch bugs!

Have Fun!

BUG JOURNAL

DATE:		TIME:		SEASON:	○ SPRING ○ SUMMER ○ FALL ○ WINTER
WEATHER CONDITIONS:		○ HOT ○ WARM ○ SUNNY ○ CLOUDY ○ RAINY ○ WINDY ○ FOGGY ○ COLD			
BUG NAME:					
WHERE DID YOU FIND IT?					
WHAT COLOR(S) IS THE BUG?					
NUMBER OF LEGS?		**DOES IT HAVE WINGS?**	○ YES ○ NO ○ NOT SURE		
NUMBER OF LEGS?					
THE BUG IS...		○ BIG ○ SHINY ○ FAST ○ SCARY ○ LITTLE ○ SLOW ○ CUTE ○ ROUND ○ THIN			
DOES IT MAKE ANY SOUND?	○ YES ○ NO	**WAS IT ALONE OR IN A GROUP?**		○ ALONE ○ GROUP	

NOTES

PHOTO/DRAWING

BUG JOURNAL

DATE:		TIME:		SEASON:	○ SPRING ○ SUMMER ○ FALL ○ WINTER

WEATHER CONDITIONS:	○ HOT ○ WARM ○ SUNNY ○ CLOUDY ○ RAINY ○ WINDY ○ FOGGY ○ COLD
BUG NAME:	
WHERE DID YOU FIND IT?	
WHAT COLOR(S) IS THE BUG?	

NUMBER OF LEGS?		DOES IT HAVE WINGS?	○ YES ○ NO ○ NOT SURE
NUMBER OF LEGS?			

THE BUG IS...	○ BIG ○ SHINY ○ FAST ○ SCARY ○ LITTLE ○ SLOW ○ CUTE ○ ROUND ○ THIN

DOES IT MAKE ANY SOUND?	○ YES ○ NO	WAS IT ALONE OR IN A GROUP?	○ ALONE ○ GROUP

NOTES

PHOTO/DRAWING

BUG JOURNAL

DATE:		TIME:		SEASON:	○ SPRING ○ SUMMER ○ FALL ○ WINTER
WEATHER CONDITIONS:		○ HOT ○ WARM ○ SUNNY ○ CLOUDY ○ RAINY ○ WINDY ○ FOGGY ○ COLD			
BUG NAME:					
WHERE DID YOU FIND IT?					
WHAT COLOR(S) IS THE BUG?					
NUMBER OF LEGS?		**DOES IT HAVE WINGS?**	○ YES ○ NO ○ NOT SURE		
NUMBER OF LEGS?					
THE BUG IS...		○ BIG ○ SHINY ○ FAST ○ SCARY ○ LITTLE ○ SLOW ○ CUTE ○ ROUND ○ THIN			
DOES IT MAKE ANY SOUND?	○ YES ○ NO	**WAS IT ALONE OR IN A GROUP?**	○ ALONE ○ GROUP		

NOTES

PHOTO/DRAWING

BUG JOURNAL

DATE:		TIME:		SEASON:	○ SPRING ○ SUMMER ○ FALL ○ WINTER

WEATHER CONDITIONS:	○ HOT ○ WARM ○ SUNNY ○ CLOUDY ○ RAINY ○ WINDY ○ FOGGY ○ COLD
BUG NAME:	
WHERE DID YOU FIND IT?	
WHAT COLOR(S) IS THE BUG?	

NUMBER OF LEGS?		DOES IT HAVE WINGS?	○ YES ○ NO ○ NOT SURE

NUMBER OF LEGS?	
THE BUG IS...	○ BIG ○ SHINY ○ FAST ○ SCARY ○ LITTLE ○ SLOW ○ CUTE ○ ROUND ○ THIN

DOES IT MAKE ANY SOUND?	○ YES ○ NO	WAS IT ALONE OR IN A GROUP?	○ ALONE ○ GROUP

NOTES

PHOTO/DRAWING

BUG JOURNAL

DATE:		TIME:		SEASON:	○ SPRING ○ SUMMER ○ FALL ○ WINTER
WEATHER CONDITIONS:		○ HOT ○ WARM ○ SUNNY ○ CLOUDY ○ RAINY ○ WINDY ○ FOGGY ○ COLD			
BUG NAME:					
WHERE DID YOU FIND IT?					
WHAT COLOR(S) IS THE BUG?					
NUMBER OF LEGS?		**DOES IT HAVE WINGS?**	○ YES ○ NO ○ NOT SURE		
NUMBER OF LEGS?					
THE BUG IS...		○ BIG ○ SHINY ○ FAST ○ SCARY ○ LITTLE ○ SLOW ○ CUTE ○ ROUND ○ THIN			
DOES IT MAKE ANY SOUND?	○ YES ○ NO	**WAS IT ALONE OR IN A GROUP?**	○ ALONE ○ GROUP		

NOTES

PHOTO/DRAWING

BUG JOURNAL

DATE:		TIME:		SEASON:	○ SPRING ○ SUMMER ○ FALL ○ WINTER

WEATHER CONDITIONS:	○ HOT ○ WARM ○ SUNNY ○ CLOUDY ○ RAINY ○ WINDY ○ FOGGY ○ COLD
BUG NAME:	
WHERE DID YOU FIND IT?	
WHAT COLOR(S) IS THE BUG?	

NUMBER OF LEGS?		DOES IT HAVE WINGS?	○ YES ○ NO ○ NOT SURE

NUMBER OF LEGS?	
THE BUG IS...	○ BIG ○ SHINY ○ FAST ○ SCARY ○ LITTLE ○ SLOW ○ CUTE ○ ROUND ○ THIN

DOES IT MAKE ANY SOUND?	○ YES ○ NO	WAS IT ALONE OR IN A GROUP?	○ ALONE ○ GROUP

NOTES

PHOTO/DRAWING

BUG JOURNAL

DATE:		TIME:		SEASON:	○ SPRING ○ SUMMER ○ FALL ○ WINTER

WEATHER CONDITIONS:	○ HOT ○ WARM ○ SUNNY ○ CLOUDY ○ RAINY ○ WINDY ○ FOGGY ○ COLD
BUG NAME:	
WHERE DID YOU FIND IT?	
WHAT COLOR(S) IS THE BUG?	

NUMBER OF LEGS?		DOES IT HAVE WINGS?	○ YES ○ NO ○ NOT SURE
NUMBER OF LEGS?			

THE BUG IS...	○ BIG ○ SHINY ○ FAST ○ SCARY ○ LITTLE ○ SLOW ○ CUTE ○ ROUND ○ THIN

DOES IT MAKE ANY SOUND?	○ YES ○ NO	WAS IT ALONE OR IN A GROUP?	○ ALONE ○ GROUP

NOTES

PHOTO/DRAWING

BUG JOURNAL

DATE:		TIME:		SEASON:	○ SPRING ○ SUMMER ○ FALL ○ WINTER

WEATHER CONDITIONS:	○ HOT ○ WARM ○ SUNNY ○ CLOUDY ○ RAINY ○ WINDY ○ FOGGY ○ COLD
BUG NAME:	
WHERE DID YOU FIND IT?	
WHAT COLOR(S) IS THE BUG?	

NUMBER OF LEGS?		DOES IT HAVE WINGS?	○ YES ○ NO ○ NOT SURE
NUMBER OF LEGS?			

THE BUG IS...	○ BIG ○ SHINY ○ FAST ○ SCARY ○ LITTLE ○ SLOW ○ CUTE ○ ROUND ○ THIN

DOES IT MAKE ANY SOUND?	○ YES ○ NO	WAS IT ALONE OR IN A GROUP?	○ ALONE ○ GROUP

NOTES

PHOTO/DRAWING

BUG JOURNAL

DATE:		TIME:		SEASON:	○ SPRING ○ SUMMER ○ FALL ○ WINTER
WEATHER CONDITIONS:		○ HOT ○ WARM ○ SUNNY ○ CLOUDY ○ RAINY ○ WINDY ○ FOGGY ○ COLD			
BUG NAME:					
WHERE DID YOU FIND IT?					
WHAT COLOR(S) IS THE BUG?					
NUMBER OF LEGS?		**DOES IT HAVE WINGS?**	○ YES ○ NO ○ NOT SURE		
NUMBER OF LEGS?					
THE BUG IS...		○ BIG ○ SHINY ○ FAST ○ SCARY ○ LITTLE ○ SLOW ○ CUTE ○ ROUND ○ THIN			
DOES IT MAKE ANY SOUND?	○ YES ○ NO	**WAS IT ALONE OR IN A GROUP?**	○ ALONE ○ GROUP		

NOTES

PHOTO/DRAWING

BUG JOURNAL

DATE:		TIME:		SEASON:	○ SPRING ○ SUMMER ○ FALL ○ WINTER

WEATHER CONDITIONS:	○ HOT ○ WARM ○ SUNNY ○ CLOUDY ○ RAINY ○ WINDY ○ FOGGY ○ COLD
BUG NAME:	
WHERE DID YOU FIND IT?	
WHAT COLOR(S) IS THE BUG?	

NUMBER OF LEGS?		DOES IT HAVE WINGS?	○ YES ○ NO ○ NOT SURE

NUMBER OF LEGS?	
THE BUG IS...	○ BIG ○ SHINY ○ FAST ○ SCARY ○ LITTLE ○ SLOW ○ CUTE ○ ROUND ○ THIN

DOES IT MAKE ANY SOUND?	○ YES ○ NO	WAS IT ALONE OR IN A GROUP?	○ ALONE ○ GROUP

NOTES

PHOTO/DRAWING

BUG JOURNAL

DATE:		TIME:		SEASON:	○ SPRING ○ SUMMER ○ FALL ○ WINTER
WEATHER CONDITIONS:		○ HOT ○ WARM ○ SUNNY ○ CLOUDY ○ RAINY ○ WINDY ○ FOGGY ○ COLD			
BUG NAME:					
WHERE DID YOU FIND IT?					
WHAT COLOR(S) IS THE BUG?					
NUMBER OF LEGS?		DOES IT HAVE WINGS?	○ YES ○ NO ○ NOT SURE		
NUMBER OF LEGS?					
THE BUG IS...		○ BIG ○ SHINY ○ FAST ○ SCARY ○ LITTLE ○ SLOW ○ CUTE ○ ROUND ○ THIN			
DOES IT MAKE ANY SOUND?	○ YES ○ NO	WAS IT ALONE OR IN A GROUP?	○ ALONE ○ GROUP		

NOTES

PHOTO/DRAWING

BUG JOURNAL

DATE:		TIME:		SEASON:	○ SPRING ○ SUMMER ○ FALL ○ WINTER
WEATHER CONDITIONS:		○ HOT ○ WARM ○ SUNNY ○ CLOUDY ○ RAINY ○ WINDY ○ FOGGY ○ COLD			
BUG NAME:					
WHERE DID YOU FIND IT?					
WHAT COLOR(S) IS THE BUG?					
NUMBER OF LEGS?		**DOES IT HAVE WINGS?**	○ YES ○ NO ○ NOT SURE		
NUMBER OF LEGS?					
THE BUG IS...		○ BIG ○ SHINY ○ FAST ○ SCARY ○ LITTLE ○ SLOW ○ CUTE ○ ROUND ○ THIN			
DOES IT MAKE ANY SOUND?	○ YES ○ NO	**WAS IT ALONE OR IN A GROUP?**	○ ALONE ○ GROUP		

NOTES

PHOTO/DRAWING

BUG JOURNAL

DATE:		TIME:		SEASON:	○ SPRING ○ SUMMER ○ FALL ○ WINTER

WEATHER CONDITIONS:	○ HOT ○ WARM ○ SUNNY ○ CLOUDY ○ RAINY ○ WINDY ○ FOGGY ○ COLD
BUG NAME:	
WHERE DID YOU FIND IT?	
WHAT COLOR(S) IS THE BUG?	

NUMBER OF LEGS?		DOES IT HAVE WINGS?	○ YES ○ NO ○ NOT SURE

NUMBER OF LEGS?	
THE BUG IS...	○ BIG ○ SHINY ○ FAST ○ SCARY ○ LITTLE ○ SLOW ○ CUTE ○ ROUND ○ THIN

DOES IT MAKE ANY SOUND?	○ YES ○ NO	WAS IT ALONE OR IN A GROUP?	○ ALONE ○ GROUP

NOTES

PHOTO/DRAWING

BUG JOURNAL

DATE:		TIME:		SEASON:	○ SPRING ○ SUMMER ○ FALL ○ WINTER

WEATHER CONDITIONS:	○ HOT ○ WARM ○ SUNNY ○ CLOUDY ○ RAINY ○ WINDY ○ FOGGY ○ COLD
BUG NAME:	
WHERE DID YOU FIND IT?	
WHAT COLOR(S) IS THE BUG?	

NUMBER OF LEGS?		DOES IT HAVE WINGS?	○ YES ○ NO ○ NOT SURE

NUMBER OF LEGS?	
THE BUG IS...	○ BIG ○ SHINY ○ FAST ○ SCARY ○ LITTLE ○ SLOW ○ CUTE ○ ROUND ○ THIN

DOES IT MAKE ANY SOUND?	○ YES ○ NO	WAS IT ALONE OR IN A GROUP?	○ ALONE ○ GROUP

NOTES

PHOTO/DRAWING

BUG JOURNAL

DATE:		TIME:		SEASON:	○ SPRING ○ SUMMER ○ FALL ○ WINTER

WEATHER CONDITIONS:	○ HOT ○ WARM ○ SUNNY ○ CLOUDY ○ RAINY ○ WINDY ○ FOGGY ○ COLD
BUG NAME:	
WHERE DID YOU FIND IT?	
WHAT COLOR(S) IS THE BUG?	

NUMBER OF LEGS?		DOES IT HAVE WINGS?	○ YES ○ NO ○ NOT SURE

NUMBER OF LEGS?	
THE BUG IS...	○ BIG ○ SHINY ○ FAST ○ SCARY ○ LITTLE ○ SLOW ○ CUTE ○ ROUND ○ THIN

DOES IT MAKE ANY SOUND?	○ YES ○ NO	WAS IT ALONE OR IN A GROUP?	○ ALONE ○ GROUP

NOTES

PHOTO/DRAWING

BUG JOURNAL

DATE:		TIME:		SEASON:	○ SPRING ○ SUMMER ○ FALL ○ WINTER

WEATHER CONDITIONS:	○ HOT ○ WARM ○ SUNNY ○ CLOUDY ○ RAINY ○ WINDY ○ FOGGY ○ COLD
BUG NAME:	
WHERE DID YOU FIND IT?	
WHAT COLOR(S) IS THE BUG?	

NUMBER OF LEGS?		DOES IT HAVE WINGS?	○ YES ○ NO ○ NOT SURE

NUMBER OF LEGS?	
THE BUG IS...	○ BIG ○ SHINY ○ FAST ○ SCARY ○ LITTLE ○ SLOW ○ CUTE ○ ROUND ○ THIN

DOES IT MAKE ANY SOUND?	○ YES ○ NO	WAS IT ALONE OR IN A GROUP?	○ ALONE ○ GROUP

NOTES

PHOTO/DRAWING

BUG JOURNAL

DATE:		TIME:		SEASON:	○ SPRING ○ SUMMER ○ FALL ○ WINTER
WEATHER CONDITIONS:		○ HOT ○ WARM ○ SUNNY ○ CLOUDY ○ RAINY ○ WINDY ○ FOGGY ○ COLD			
BUG NAME:					
WHERE DID YOU FIND IT?					
WHAT COLOR(S) IS THE BUG?					
NUMBER OF LEGS?		**DOES IT HAVE WINGS?**	○ YES ○ NO ○ NOT SURE		
NUMBER OF LEGS?					
THE BUG IS...		○ BIG ○ SHINY ○ FAST ○ SCARY ○ LITTLE ○ SLOW ○ CUTE ○ ROUND ○ THIN			
DOES IT MAKE ANY SOUND?	○ YES ○ NO	**WAS IT ALONE OR IN A GROUP?**	○ ALONE ○ GROUP		

NOTES

PHOTO/DRAWING

BUG JOURNAL

DATE:		TIME:		SEASON:	○ SPRING ○ SUMMER ○ FALL ○ WINTER

WEATHER CONDITIONS:	○ HOT ○ WARM ○ SUNNY ○ CLOUDY ○ RAINY ○ WINDY ○ FOGGY ○ COLD

BUG NAME:	
WHERE DID YOU FIND IT?	
WHAT COLOR(S) IS THE BUG?	

NUMBER OF LEGS?		DOES IT HAVE WINGS?	○ YES ○ NO ○ NOT SURE
NUMBER OF LEGS?			

THE BUG IS...	○ BIG ○ SHINY ○ FAST ○ SCARY ○ LITTLE ○ SLOW ○ CUTE ○ ROUND ○ THIN

DOES IT MAKE ANY SOUND?	○ YES ○ NO	WAS IT ALONE OR IN A GROUP?	○ ALONE ○ GROUP

NOTES

PHOTO/DRAWING

BUG JOURNAL

DATE:		TIME:		SEASON:	○ SPRING ○ SUMMER ○ FALL ○ WINTER

WEATHER CONDITIONS:	○ HOT ○ WARM ○ SUNNY ○ CLOUDY ○ RAINY ○ WINDY ○ FOGGY ○ COLD
BUG NAME:	
WHERE DID YOU FIND IT?	
WHAT COLOR(S) IS THE BUG?	

NUMBER OF LEGS?		DOES IT HAVE WINGS?	○ YES ○ NO ○ NOT SURE

NUMBER OF LEGS?	
THE BUG IS...	○ BIG ○ SHINY ○ FAST ○ SCARY ○ LITTLE ○ SLOW ○ CUTE ○ ROUND ○ THIN

DOES IT MAKE ANY SOUND?	○ YES ○ NO	WAS IT ALONE OR IN A GROUP?	○ ALONE ○ GROUP

NOTES

PHOTO/DRAWING

BUG JOURNAL

DATE:		TIME:		SEASON:	○ SPRING ○ SUMMER ○ FALL ○ WINTER

WEATHER CONDITIONS:	○ HOT ○ WARM ○ SUNNY ○ CLOUDY ○ RAINY ○ WINDY ○ FOGGY ○ COLD
BUG NAME:	
WHERE DID YOU FIND IT?	
WHAT COLOR(S) IS THE BUG?	

NUMBER OF LEGS?		DOES IT HAVE WINGS?	○ YES ○ NO ○ NOT SURE

NUMBER OF LEGS?	
THE BUG IS...	○ BIG ○ SHINY ○ FAST ○ SCARY ○ LITTLE ○ SLOW ○ CUTE ○ ROUND ○ THIN

DOES IT MAKE ANY SOUND?	○ YES ○ NO	WAS IT ALONE OR IN A GROUP?	○ ALONE ○ GROUP

NOTES

PHOTO/DRAWING

BUG JOURNAL

DATE:		TIME:		SEASON:	○ SPRING ○ SUMMER ○ FALL ○ WINTER

WEATHER CONDITIONS:	○ HOT ○ WARM ○ SUNNY ○ CLOUDY ○ RAINY ○ WINDY ○ FOGGY ○ COLD

BUG NAME:	
WHERE DID YOU FIND IT?	
WHAT COLOR(S) IS THE BUG?	

NUMBER OF LEGS?		DOES IT HAVE WINGS?	○ YES ○ NO ○ NOT SURE

NUMBER OF LEGS?	

THE BUG IS...	○ BIG ○ SHINY ○ FAST ○ SCARY ○ LITTLE ○ SLOW ○ CUTE ○ ROUND ○ THIN

DOES IT MAKE ANY SOUND?	○ YES ○ NO	WAS IT ALONE OR IN A GROUP?	○ ALONE ○ GROUP

NOTES

PHOTO/DRAWING

BUG JOURNAL

DATE:		TIME:		SEASON:	○ SPRING ○ SUMMER ○ FALL ○ WINTER

WEATHER CONDITIONS:	○ HOT ○ WARM ○ SUNNY ○ CLOUDY ○ RAINY ○ WINDY ○ FOGGY ○ COLD
BUG NAME:	
WHERE DID YOU FIND IT?	
WHAT COLOR(S) IS THE BUG?	

NUMBER OF LEGS?		DOES IT HAVE WINGS?	○ YES ○ NO ○ NOT SURE

NUMBER OF LEGS?	
THE BUG IS...	○ BIG ○ SHINY ○ FAST ○ SCARY ○ LITTLE ○ SLOW ○ CUTE ○ ROUND ○ THIN

DOES IT MAKE ANY SOUND?	○ YES ○ NO	WAS IT ALONE OR IN A GROUP?	○ ALONE ○ GROUP

NOTES

PHOTO/DRAWING

BUG JOURNAL

DATE:		TIME:		SEASON:	○ SPRING ○ SUMMER ○ FALL ○ WINTER

WEATHER CONDITIONS:	○ HOT ○ WARM ○ SUNNY ○ CLOUDY ○ RAINY ○ WINDY ○ FOGGY ○ COLD
BUG NAME:	
WHERE DID YOU FIND IT?	
WHAT COLOR(S) IS THE BUG?	

NUMBER OF LEGS?		DOES IT HAVE WINGS?	○ YES ○ NO ○ NOT SURE

NUMBER OF LEGS?	
THE BUG IS...	○ BIG ○ SHINY ○ FAST ○ SCARY ○ LITTLE ○ SLOW ○ CUTE ○ ROUND ○ THIN

DOES IT MAKE ANY SOUND?	○ YES ○ NO	WAS IT ALONE OR IN A GROUP?	○ ALONE ○ GROUP

NOTES

PHOTO/DRAWING

BUG JOURNAL

DATE:		TIME:		SEASON:	○ SPRING ○ SUMMER ○ FALL ○ WINTER

WEATHER CONDITIONS:	○ HOT ○ WARM ○ SUNNY ○ CLOUDY ○ RAINY ○ WINDY ○ FOGGY ○ COLD
BUG NAME:	
WHERE DID YOU FIND IT?	
WHAT COLOR(S) IS THE BUG?	

NUMBER OF LEGS?		DOES IT HAVE WINGS?	○ YES ○ NO ○ NOT SURE

NUMBER OF LEGS?	
THE BUG IS...	○ BIG ○ SHINY ○ FAST ○ SCARY ○ LITTLE ○ SLOW ○ CUTE ○ ROUND ○ THIN

DOES IT MAKE ANY SOUND?	○ YES ○ NO	WAS IT ALONE OR IN A GROUP?	○ ALONE ○ GROUP

NOTES

PHOTO/DRAWING

BUG JOURNAL

DATE:		TIME:		SEASON:	○ SPRING ○ SUMMER ○ FALL ○ WINTER
WEATHER CONDITIONS:		○ HOT ○ WARM ○ SUNNY ○ CLOUDY ○ RAINY ○ WINDY ○ FOGGY ○ COLD			
BUG NAME:					
WHERE DID YOU FIND IT?					
WHAT COLOR(S) IS THE BUG?					
NUMBER OF LEGS?		**DOES IT HAVE WINGS?**	○ YES ○ NO ○ NOT SURE		
NUMBER OF LEGS?					
THE BUG IS...		○ BIG ○ SHINY ○ FAST ○ SCARY ○ LITTLE ○ SLOW ○ CUTE ○ ROUND ○ THIN			
DOES IT MAKE ANY SOUND?	○ YES ○ NO	**WAS IT ALONE OR IN A GROUP?**	○ ALONE ○ GROUP		

NOTES

PHOTO/DRAWING

BUG JOURNAL

DATE:		TIME:		SEASON:	○ SPRING ○ SUMMER ○ FALL ○ WINTER
WEATHER CONDITIONS:		○ HOT ○ WARM ○ SUNNY ○ CLOUDY ○ RAINY ○ WINDY ○ FOGGY ○ COLD			
BUG NAME:					
WHERE DID YOU FIND IT?					
WHAT COLOR(S) IS THE BUG?					
NUMBER OF LEGS?		**DOES IT HAVE WINGS?**	○ YES ○ NO ○ NOT SURE		
NUMBER OF LEGS?					
THE BUG IS...		○ BIG ○ SHINY ○ FAST ○ SCARY ○ LITTLE ○ SLOW ○ CUTE ○ ROUND ○ THIN			
DOES IT MAKE ANY SOUND?	○ YES ○ NO	**WAS IT ALONE OR IN A GROUP?**	○ ALONE ○ GROUP		

NOTES

PHOTO/DRAWING

BUG JOURNAL

DATE:		TIME:		SEASON:	○ SPRING ○ SUMMER ○ FALL ○ WINTER

WEATHER CONDITIONS:	○ HOT ○ WARM ○ SUNNY ○ CLOUDY ○ RAINY ○ WINDY ○ FOGGY ○ COLD
BUG NAME:	
WHERE DID YOU FIND IT?	
WHAT COLOR(S) IS THE BUG?	

NUMBER OF LEGS?		DOES IT HAVE WINGS?	○ YES ○ NO ○ NOT SURE

NUMBER OF LEGS?	
THE BUG IS...	○ BIG ○ SHINY ○ FAST ○ SCARY ○ LITTLE ○ SLOW ○ CUTE ○ ROUND ○ THIN

DOES IT MAKE ANY SOUND?	○ YES ○ NO	WAS IT ALONE OR IN A GROUP?	○ ALONE ○ GROUP

NOTES

PHOTO/DRAWING

BUG JOURNAL

DATE:		TIME:		SEASON:	○ SPRING ○ SUMMER ○ FALL ○ WINTER

WEATHER CONDITIONS:	○ HOT ○ WARM ○ SUNNY ○ CLOUDY ○ RAINY ○ WINDY ○ FOGGY ○ COLD
BUG NAME:	
WHERE DID YOU FIND IT?	
WHAT COLOR(S) IS THE BUG?	

NUMBER OF LEGS?		DOES IT HAVE WINGS?	○ YES ○ NO ○ NOT SURE

NUMBER OF LEGS?	
THE BUG IS...	○ BIG ○ SHINY ○ FAST ○ SCARY ○ LITTLE ○ SLOW ○ CUTE ○ ROUND ○ THIN

DOES IT MAKE ANY SOUND?	○ YES ○ NO	WAS IT ALONE OR IN A GROUP?	○ ALONE ○ GROUP

NOTES

PHOTO/DRAWING

BUG JOURNAL

DATE:		TIME:		SEASON:	○ SPRING ○ SUMMER ○ FALL ○ WINTER
WEATHER CONDITIONS:		○ HOT ○ WARM ○ SUNNY ○ CLOUDY ○ RAINY ○ WINDY ○ FOGGY ○ COLD			
BUG NAME:					
WHERE DID YOU FIND IT?					
WHAT COLOR(S) IS THE BUG?					
NUMBER OF LEGS?		DOES IT HAVE WINGS?	○ YES ○ NO ○ NOT SURE		
NUMBER OF LEGS?					
THE BUG IS...		○ BIG ○ SHINY ○ FAST ○ SCARY ○ LITTLE ○ SLOW ○ CUTE ○ ROUND ○ THIN			
DOES IT MAKE ANY SOUND?	○ YES ○ NO	WAS IT ALONE OR IN A GROUP?	○ ALONE ○ GROUP		

NOTES

PHOTO/DRAWING

BUG JOURNAL

DATE:		TIME:		SEASON:	○ SPRING ○ SUMMER ○ FALL ○ WINTER

WEATHER CONDITIONS:	○ HOT ○ WARM ○ SUNNY ○ CLOUDY ○ RAINY ○ WINDY ○ FOGGY ○ COLD
BUG NAME:	
WHERE DID YOU FIND IT?	
WHAT COLOR(S) IS THE BUG?	

NUMBER OF LEGS?		DOES IT HAVE WINGS?	○ YES ○ NO ○ NOT SURE

NUMBER OF LEGS?	
THE BUG IS...	○ BIG ○ SHINY ○ FAST ○ SCARY ○ LITTLE ○ SLOW ○ CUTE ○ ROUND ○ THIN

DOES IT MAKE ANY SOUND?	○ YES ○ NO	WAS IT ALONE OR IN A GROUP?	○ ALONE ○ GROUP

NOTES

PHOTO/DRAWING

BUG JOURNAL

DATE:			TIME:		SEASON:	○ SPRING ○ SUMMER ○ FALL ○ WINTER
WEATHER CONDITIONS:			○ HOT ○ WARM ○ SUNNY ○ CLOUDY ○ RAINY ○ WINDY ○ FOGGY ○ COLD			
BUG NAME:						
WHERE DID YOU FIND IT?						
WHAT COLOR(S) IS THE BUG?						
NUMBER OF LEGS?			DOES IT HAVE WINGS?	○ YES ○ NO ○ NOT SURE		
NUMBER OF LEGS?						
THE BUG IS...			○ BIG ○ SHINY ○ FAST ○ SCARY ○ LITTLE ○ SLOW ○ CUTE ○ ROUND ○ THIN			
DOES IT MAKE ANY SOUND?	○ YES ○ NO	WAS IT ALONE OR IN A GROUP?	○ ALONE ○ GROUP			

NOTES

PHOTO/DRAWING

BUG JOURNAL

DATE:		TIME:		SEASON:	○ SPRING ○ SUMMER ○ FALL ○ WINTER

WEATHER CONDITIONS:	○ HOT ○ WARM ○ SUNNY ○ CLOUDY ○ RAINY ○ WINDY ○ FOGGY ○ COLD
BUG NAME:	
WHERE DID YOU FIND IT?	
WHAT COLOR(S) IS THE BUG?	

NUMBER OF LEGS?		DOES IT HAVE WINGS?	○ YES ○ NO ○ NOT SURE

NUMBER OF LEGS?	
THE BUG IS...	○ BIG ○ SHINY ○ FAST ○ SCARY ○ LITTLE ○ SLOW ○ CUTE ○ ROUND ○ THIN

DOES IT MAKE ANY SOUND?	○ YES ○ NO	WAS IT ALONE OR IN A GROUP?	○ ALONE ○ GROUP

NOTES

PHOTO/DRAWING

BUG JOURNAL

DATE:		TIME:		SEASON:	○ SPRING ○ SUMMER ○ FALL ○ WINTER

WEATHER CONDITIONS:	○ HOT ○ WARM ○ SUNNY ○ CLOUDY ○ RAINY ○ WINDY ○ FOGGY ○ COLD
BUG NAME:	
WHERE DID YOU FIND IT?	
WHAT COLOR(S) IS THE BUG?	

NUMBER OF LEGS?		DOES IT HAVE WINGS?	○ YES ○ NO ○ NOT SURE
NUMBER OF LEGS?			

THE BUG IS...	○ BIG ○ SHINY ○ FAST ○ SCARY ○ LITTLE ○ SLOW ○ CUTE ○ ROUND ○ THIN

DOES IT MAKE ANY SOUND?	○ YES ○ NO	WAS IT ALONE OR IN A GROUP?	○ ALONE ○ GROUP

NOTES

PHOTO/DRAWING

BUG JOURNAL

DATE:		TIME:		SEASON:	○ SPRING ○ SUMMER ○ FALL ○ WINTER

WEATHER CONDITIONS:	○ HOT ○ WARM ○ SUNNY ○ CLOUDY ○ RAINY ○ WINDY ○ FOGGY ○ COLD
BUG NAME:	
WHERE DID YOU FIND IT?	
WHAT COLOR(S) IS THE BUG?	

NUMBER OF LEGS?		DOES IT HAVE WINGS?	○ YES ○ NO ○ NOT SURE

NUMBER OF LEGS?	
THE BUG IS...	○ BIG ○ SHINY ○ FAST ○ SCARY ○ LITTLE ○ SLOW ○ CUTE ○ ROUND ○ THIN

DOES IT MAKE ANY SOUND?	○ YES ○ NO	WAS IT ALONE OR IN A GROUP?	○ ALONE ○ GROUP

NOTES

PHOTO/DRAWING

BUG JOURNAL

DATE:		TIME:		SEASON:	○ SPRING ○ SUMMER ○ FALL ○ WINTER
WEATHER CONDITIONS:		○ HOT ○ WARM ○ SUNNY ○ CLOUDY ○ RAINY ○ WINDY ○ FOGGY ○ COLD			
BUG NAME:					
WHERE DID YOU FIND IT?					
WHAT COLOR(S) IS THE BUG?					
NUMBER OF LEGS?		DOES IT HAVE WINGS?	○ YES ○ NO ○ NOT SURE		
NUMBER OF LEGS?					
THE BUG IS...		○ BIG ○ SHINY ○ FAST ○ SCARY ○ LITTLE ○ SLOW ○ CUTE ○ ROUND ○ THIN			
DOES IT MAKE ANY SOUND?	○ YES ○ NO	WAS IT ALONE OR IN A GROUP?		○ ALONE ○ GROUP	

NOTES

PHOTO/DRAWING

BUG JOURNAL

DATE:		TIME:		SEASON:	○ SPRING ○ SUMMER ○ FALL ○ WINTER

WEATHER CONDITIONS:	○ HOT ○ WARM ○ SUNNY ○ CLOUDY ○ RAINY ○ WINDY ○ FOGGY ○ COLD
BUG NAME:	
WHERE DID YOU FIND IT?	
WHAT COLOR(S) IS THE BUG?	

NUMBER OF LEGS?		DOES IT HAVE WINGS?	○ YES ○ NO ○ NOT SURE
NUMBER OF LEGS?			
THE BUG IS...	○ BIG ○ SHINY ○ FAST ○ SCARY ○ LITTLE ○ SLOW ○ CUTE ○ ROUND ○ THIN		

DOES IT MAKE ANY SOUND?	○ YES ○ NO	WAS IT ALONE OR IN A GROUP?	○ ALONE ○ GROUP

NOTES

PHOTO/DRAWING

BUG JOURNAL

DATE:		TIME:		SEASON:	○ SPRING ○ SUMMER ○ FALL ○ WINTER

WEATHER CONDITIONS:	○ HOT ○ WARM ○ SUNNY ○ CLOUDY ○ RAINY ○ WINDY ○ FOGGY ○ COLD
BUG NAME:	
WHERE DID YOU FIND IT?	
WHAT COLOR(S) IS THE BUG?	

NUMBER OF LEGS?		DOES IT HAVE WINGS?	○ YES ○ NO ○ NOT SURE

NUMBER OF LEGS?	
THE BUG IS...	○ BIG ○ SHINY ○ FAST ○ SCARY ○ LITTLE ○ SLOW ○ CUTE ○ ROUND ○ THIN

DOES IT MAKE ANY SOUND?	○ YES ○ NO	WAS IT ALONE OR IN A GROUP?	○ ALONE ○ GROUP

NOTES

PHOTO/DRAWING

BUG JOURNAL

DATE:		TIME:		SEASON:	○ SPRING ○ SUMMER ○ FALL ○ WINTER

WEATHER CONDITIONS:	○ HOT ○ WARM ○ SUNNY ○ CLOUDY ○ RAINY ○ WINDY ○ FOGGY ○ COLD
BUG NAME:	
WHERE DID YOU FIND IT?	
WHAT COLOR(S) IS THE BUG?	

NUMBER OF LEGS?		DOES IT HAVE WINGS?	○ YES ○ NO ○ NOT SURE
NUMBER OF LEGS?			

THE BUG IS...	○ BIG ○ SHINY ○ FAST ○ SCARY ○ LITTLE ○ SLOW ○ CUTE ○ ROUND ○ THIN

DOES IT MAKE ANY SOUND?	○ YES ○ NO	WAS IT ALONE OR IN A GROUP?	○ ALONE ○ GROUP

NOTES

PHOTO/DRAWING

BUG JOURNAL

DATE:		TIME:		SEASON:	○ SPRING ○ SUMMER ○ FALL ○ WINTER

WEATHER CONDITIONS:	○ HOT ○ WARM ○ SUNNY ○ CLOUDY ○ RAINY ○ WINDY ○ FOGGY ○ COLD
BUG NAME:	
WHERE DID YOU FIND IT?	
WHAT COLOR(S) IS THE BUG?	

NUMBER OF LEGS?		DOES IT HAVE WINGS?	○ YES ○ NO ○ NOT SURE

NUMBER OF LEGS?	
THE BUG IS...	○ BIG ○ SHINY ○ FAST ○ SCARY ○ LITTLE ○ SLOW ○ CUTE ○ ROUND ○ THIN

DOES IT MAKE ANY SOUND?	○ YES ○ NO	WAS IT ALONE OR IN A GROUP?	○ ALONE ○ GROUP

NOTES

PHOTO/DRAWING

BUG JOURNAL

DATE:		TIME:		SEASON:	○ SPRING ○ SUMMER ○ FALL ○ WINTER

WEATHER CONDITIONS:	○ HOT ○ WARM ○ SUNNY ○ CLOUDY ○ RAINY ○ WINDY ○ FOGGY ○ COLD
BUG NAME:	
WHERE DID YOU FIND IT?	
WHAT COLOR(S) IS THE BUG?	

NUMBER OF LEGS?		DOES IT HAVE WINGS?	○ YES ○ NO ○ NOT SURE

NUMBER OF LEGS?	
THE BUG IS...	○ BIG ○ SHINY ○ FAST ○ SCARY ○ LITTLE ○ SLOW ○ CUTE ○ ROUND ○ THIN

DOES IT MAKE ANY SOUND?	○ YES ○ NO	WAS IT ALONE OR IN A GROUP?	○ ALONE ○ GROUP

NOTES

PHOTO/DRAWING

BUG JOURNAL

DATE:		TIME:		SEASON:	○ SPRING ○ SUMMER ○ FALL ○ WINTER

WEATHER CONDITIONS:	○ HOT ○ WARM ○ SUNNY ○ CLOUDY ○ RAINY ○ WINDY ○ FOGGY ○ COLD
BUG NAME:	
WHERE DID YOU FIND IT?	
WHAT COLOR(S) IS THE BUG?	

NUMBER OF LEGS?		DOES IT HAVE WINGS?	○ YES ○ NO ○ NOT SURE

NUMBER OF LEGS?	
THE BUG IS...	○ BIG ○ SHINY ○ FAST ○ SCARY ○ LITTLE ○ SLOW ○ CUTE ○ ROUND ○ THIN

DOES IT MAKE ANY SOUND?	○ YES ○ NO	WAS IT ALONE OR IN A GROUP?	○ ALONE ○ GROUP

NOTES

PHOTO/DRAWING

BUG JOURNAL

DATE:		TIME:		SEASON:	○ SPRING ○ SUMMER ○ FALL ○ WINTER
WEATHER CONDITIONS:		○ HOT ○ WARM ○ SUNNY ○ CLOUDY ○ RAINY ○ WINDY ○ FOGGY ○ COLD			
BUG NAME:					
WHERE DID YOU FIND IT?					
WHAT COLOR(S) IS THE BUG?					
NUMBER OF LEGS?		DOES IT HAVE WINGS?	○ YES ○ NO ○ NOT SURE		
NUMBER OF LEGS?					
THE BUG IS...		○ BIG ○ SHINY ○ FAST ○ SCARY ○ LITTLE ○ SLOW ○ CUTE ○ ROUND ○ THIN			
DOES IT MAKE ANY SOUND?	○ YES ○ NO	WAS IT ALONE OR IN A GROUP?	○ ALONE ○ GROUP		

NOTES

PHOTO/DRAWING

BUG JOURNAL

DATE:		TIME:		SEASON:	○ SPRING ○ SUMMER ○ FALL ○ WINTER
WEATHER CONDITIONS:		○ HOT ○ WARM ○ SUNNY ○ CLOUDY ○ RAINY ○ WINDY ○ FOGGY ○ COLD			
BUG NAME:					
WHERE DID YOU FIND IT?					
WHAT COLOR(S) IS THE BUG?					
NUMBER OF LEGS?		**DOES IT HAVE WINGS?**	○ YES ○ NO ○ NOT SURE		
NUMBER OF LEGS?					
THE BUG IS...		○ BIG ○ SHINY ○ FAST ○ SCARY ○ LITTLE ○ SLOW ○ CUTE ○ ROUND ○ THIN			
DOES IT MAKE ANY SOUND?	○ YES ○ NO	**WAS IT ALONE OR IN A GROUP?**	○ ALONE ○ GROUP		

NOTES

PHOTO/DRAWING

BUG JOURNAL

DATE:		TIME:		SEASON:	○ SPRING ○ SUMMER ○ FALL ○ WINTER

WEATHER CONDITIONS:	○ HOT ○ WARM ○ SUNNY ○ CLOUDY ○ RAINY ○ WINDY ○ FOGGY ○ COLD
BUG NAME:	
WHERE DID YOU FIND IT?	
WHAT COLOR(S) IS THE BUG?	

NUMBER OF LEGS?		DOES IT HAVE WINGS?	○ YES ○ NO ○ NOT SURE

NUMBER OF LEGS?	
THE BUG IS...	○ BIG ○ SHINY ○ FAST ○ SCARY ○ LITTLE ○ SLOW ○ CUTE ○ ROUND ○ THIN

DOES IT MAKE ANY SOUND?	○ YES ○ NO	WAS IT ALONE OR IN A GROUP?	○ ALONE ○ GROUP

NOTES

PHOTO/DRAWING

BUG JOURNAL

DATE:		TIME:		SEASON:	○ SPRING ○ SUMMER ○ FALL ○ WINTER

WEATHER CONDITIONS:	○ HOT ○ WARM ○ SUNNY ○ CLOUDY ○ RAINY ○ WINDY ○ FOGGY ○ COLD
BUG NAME:	
WHERE DID YOU FIND IT?	
WHAT COLOR(S) IS THE BUG?	

NUMBER OF LEGS?		DOES IT HAVE WINGS?	○ YES ○ NO ○ NOT SURE
NUMBER OF LEGS?			

THE BUG IS...	○ BIG ○ SHINY ○ FAST ○ SCARY ○ LITTLE ○ SLOW ○ CUTE ○ ROUND ○ THIN

DOES IT MAKE ANY SOUND?	○ YES ○ NO	WAS IT ALONE OR IN A GROUP?	○ ALONE ○ GROUP

NOTES

PHOTO/DRAWING

BUG JOURNAL

DATE:		TIME:		SEASON:	○ SPRING ○ SUMMER ○ FALL ○ WINTER

WEATHER CONDITIONS:	○ HOT ○ WARM ○ SUNNY ○ CLOUDY ○ RAINY ○ WINDY ○ FOGGY ○ COLD
BUG NAME:	
WHERE DID YOU FIND IT?	
WHAT COLOR(S) IS THE BUG?	

NUMBER OF LEGS?		DOES IT HAVE WINGS?	○ YES ○ NO ○ NOT SURE
NUMBER OF LEGS?			

THE BUG IS...	○ BIG ○ SHINY ○ FAST ○ SCARY ○ LITTLE ○ SLOW ○ CUTE ○ ROUND ○ THIN

DOES IT MAKE ANY SOUND?	○ YES ○ NO	WAS IT ALONE OR IN A GROUP?	○ ALONE ○ GROUP

NOTES

PHOTO/DRAWING

BUG JOURNAL

DATE:		TIME:		SEASON:	○ SPRING ○ SUMMER ○ FALL ○ WINTER

WEATHER CONDITIONS:	○ HOT ○ WARM ○ SUNNY ○ CLOUDY ○ RAINY ○ WINDY ○ FOGGY ○ COLD
BUG NAME:	
WHERE DID YOU FIND IT?	
WHAT COLOR(S) IS THE BUG?	

NUMBER OF LEGS?		DOES IT HAVE WINGS?	○ YES ○ NO ○ NOT SURE
NUMBER OF LEGS?			

THE BUG IS...	○ BIG ○ SHINY ○ FAST ○ SCARY ○ LITTLE ○ SLOW ○ CUTE ○ ROUND ○ THIN

DOES IT MAKE ANY SOUND?	○ YES ○ NO	WAS IT ALONE OR IN A GROUP?	○ ALONE ○ GROUP

NOTES

PHOTO/DRAWING

BUG JOURNAL

DATE:		TIME:		SEASON:	○ SPRING ○ SUMMER ○ FALL ○ WINTER

WEATHER CONDITIONS:	○ HOT ○ WARM ○ SUNNY ○ CLOUDY ○ RAINY ○ WINDY ○ FOGGY ○ COLD
BUG NAME:	
WHERE DID YOU FIND IT?	
WHAT COLOR(S) IS THE BUG?	

NUMBER OF LEGS?		DOES IT HAVE WINGS?	○ YES ○ NO ○ NOT SURE

NUMBER OF LEGS?	
THE BUG IS...	○ BIG ○ SHINY ○ FAST ○ SCARY ○ LITTLE ○ SLOW ○ CUTE ○ ROUND ○ THIN

DOES IT MAKE ANY SOUND?	○ YES ○ NO	WAS IT ALONE OR IN A GROUP?	○ ALONE ○ GROUP

NOTES

PHOTO/DRAWING

BUG JOURNAL

DATE:		TIME:		SEASON:	○ SPRING ○ SUMMER ○ FALL ○ WINTER
WEATHER CONDITIONS:		○ HOT ○ WARM ○ SUNNY ○ CLOUDY ○ RAINY ○ WINDY ○ FOGGY ○ COLD			
BUG NAME:					
WHERE DID YOU FIND IT?					
WHAT COLOR(S) IS THE BUG?					
NUMBER OF LEGS?		DOES IT HAVE WINGS?	○ YES ○ NO ○ NOT SURE		
NUMBER OF LEGS?					
THE BUG IS...		○ BIG ○ SHINY ○ FAST ○ SCARY ○ LITTLE ○ SLOW ○ CUTE ○ ROUND ○ THIN			
DOES IT MAKE ANY SOUND?	○ YES ○ NO	WAS IT ALONE OR IN A GROUP?		○ ALONE ○ GROUP	

NOTES

PHOTO/DRAWING

BUG JOURNAL

DATE:		TIME:		SEASON:	○ SPRING ○ SUMMER ○ FALL ○ WINTER

WEATHER CONDITIONS:	○ HOT ○ WARM ○ SUNNY ○ CLOUDY ○ RAINY ○ WINDY ○ FOGGY ○ COLD
BUG NAME:	
WHERE DID YOU FIND IT?	
WHAT COLOR(S) IS THE BUG?	

NUMBER OF LEGS?		DOES IT HAVE WINGS?	○ YES ○ NO ○ NOT SURE

NUMBER OF LEGS?	
THE BUG IS...	○ BIG ○ SHINY ○ FAST ○ SCARY ○ LITTLE ○ SLOW ○ CUTE ○ ROUND ○ THIN

DOES IT MAKE ANY SOUND?	○ YES ○ NO	WAS IT ALONE OR IN A GROUP?	○ ALONE ○ GROUP

NOTES

PHOTO/DRAWING

BUG JOURNAL

DATE:		TIME:		SEASON:	○ SPRING ○ SUMMER ○ FALL ○ WINTER		
WEATHER CONDITIONS:		○ HOT ○ WARM ○ SUNNY ○ CLOUDY ○ RAINY ○ WINDY ○ FOGGY ○ COLD					
BUG NAME:							
WHERE DID YOU FIND IT?							
WHAT COLOR(S) IS THE BUG?							
NUMBER OF LEGS?			**DOES IT HAVE WINGS?**		○ YES ○ NO ○ NOT SURE		
NUMBER OF LEGS?							
THE BUG IS...		○ BIG ○ SHINY ○ FAST ○ SCARY ○ LITTLE ○ SLOW ○ CUTE ○ ROUND ○ THIN					
DOES IT MAKE ANY SOUND?		○ YES ○ NO	**WAS IT ALONE OR IN A GROUP?**		○ ALONE ○ GROUP		

NOTES

PHOTO/DRAWING

BUG JOURNAL

DATE:		TIME:		SEASON:	SPRING ○ SUMMER ○ FALL ○ WINTER

WEATHER CONDITIONS:	○ HOT ○ WARM ○ SUNNY ○ CLOUDY ○ RAINY ○ WINDY ○ FOGGY ○ COLD
BUG NAME:	
WHERE DID YOU FIND IT?	
WHAT COLOR(S) IS THE BUG?	

NUMBER OF LEGS?		DOES IT HAVE WINGS?	○ YES ○ NO ○ NOT SURE

NUMBER OF LEGS?	
THE BUG IS...	○ BIG ○ SHINY ○ FAST ○ SCARY ○ LITTLE ○ SLOW ○ CUTE ○ ROUND ○ THIN

DOES IT MAKE ANY SOUND?	○ YES ○ NO	WAS IT ALONE OR IN A GROUP?	○ ALONE ○ GROUP

NOTES

PHOTO/DRAWING

BUG JOURNAL

DATE:		TIME:		SEASON:	○ SPRING ○ SUMMER ○ FALL ○ WINTER
WEATHER CONDITIONS:		○ HOT ○ WARM ○ SUNNY ○ CLOUDY ○ RAINY ○ WINDY ○ FOGGY ○ COLD				
BUG NAME:						
WHERE DID YOU FIND IT?						
WHAT COLOR(S) IS THE BUG?						
NUMBER OF LEGS?		DOES IT HAVE WINGS?	○ YES ○ NO ○ NOT SURE			
NUMBER OF LEGS?						
THE BUG IS...		○ BIG ○ SHINY ○ FAST ○ SCARY ○ LITTLE ○ SLOW ○ CUTE ○ ROUND ○ THIN				
DOES IT MAKE ANY SOUND?	○ YES ○ NO	WAS IT ALONE OR IN A GROUP?	○ ALONE ○ GROUP			

NOTES

PHOTO/DRAWING

BUG JOURNAL

DATE:			TIME:		SEASON:	○ SPRING ○ SUMMER ○ FALL ○ WINTER

WEATHER CONDITIONS:	○ HOT ○ WARM ○ SUNNY ○ CLOUDY ○ RAINY ○ WINDY ○ FOGGY ○ COLD
BUG NAME:	
WHERE DID YOU FIND IT?	
WHAT COLOR(S) IS THE BUG?	

NUMBER OF LEGS?		DOES IT HAVE WINGS?	○ YES ○ NO ○ NOT SURE

NUMBER OF LEGS?	
THE BUG IS...	○ BIG ○ SHINY ○ FAST ○ SCARY ○ LITTLE ○ SLOW ○ CUTE ○ ROUND ○ THIN

DOES IT MAKE ANY SOUND?	○ YES ○ NO	WAS IT ALONE OR IN A GROUP?	○ ALONE ○ GROUP

NOTES

PHOTO/DRAWING

BUG JOURNAL

DATE:		TIME:		SEASON:	○ SPRING ○ SUMMER ○ FALL ○ WINTER

WEATHER CONDITIONS:	○ HOT ○ WARM ○ SUNNY ○ CLOUDY ○ RAINY ○ WINDY ○ FOGGY ○ COLD
BUG NAME:	
WHERE DID YOU FIND IT?	
WHAT COLOR(S) IS THE BUG?	

NUMBER OF LEGS?		DOES IT HAVE WINGS?	○ YES ○ NO ○ NOT SURE

NUMBER OF LEGS?	
THE BUG IS...	○ BIG ○ SHINY ○ FAST ○ SCARY ○ LITTLE ○ SLOW ○ CUTE ○ ROUND ○ THIN

DOES IT MAKE ANY SOUND?	○ YES ○ NO	WAS IT ALONE OR IN A GROUP?	○ ALONE ○ GROUP

NOTES

PHOTO/DRAWING

BUG JOURNAL

DATE:		TIME:		SEASON:	○ SPRING ○ SUMMER ○ FALL ○ WINTER

WEATHER CONDITIONS:	○ HOT ○ WARM ○ SUNNY ○ CLOUDY ○ RAINY ○ WINDY ○ FOGGY ○ COLD
BUG NAME:	
WHERE DID YOU FIND IT?	
WHAT COLOR(S) IS THE BUG?	

NUMBER OF LEGS?		DOES IT HAVE WINGS?	○ YES ○ NO ○ NOT SURE

NUMBER OF LEGS?	
THE BUG IS...	○ BIG ○ SHINY ○ FAST ○ SCARY ○ LITTLE ○ SLOW ○ CUTE ○ ROUND ○ THIN

DOES IT MAKE ANY SOUND?	○ YES ○ NO	WAS IT ALONE OR IN A GROUP?	○ ALONE ○ GROUP

NOTES

PHOTO/DRAWING

BUG JOURNAL

DATE:		TIME:		SEASON:	○ SPRING ○ SUMMER ○ FALL ○ WINTER

WEATHER CONDITIONS:	○ HOT ○ WARM ○ SUNNY ○ CLOUDY ○ RAINY ○ WINDY ○ FOGGY ○ COLD
BUG NAME:	
WHERE DID YOU FIND IT?	
WHAT COLOR(S) IS THE BUG?	

NUMBER OF LEGS?		DOES IT HAVE WINGS?	○ YES ○ NO ○ NOT SURE
NUMBER OF LEGS?			

THE BUG IS...	○ BIG ○ SHINY ○ FAST ○ SCARY ○ LITTLE ○ SLOW ○ CUTE ○ ROUND ○ THIN

DOES IT MAKE ANY SOUND?	○ YES ○ NO	WAS IT ALONE OR IN A GROUP?	○ ALONE ○ GROUP

NOTES

PHOTO/DRAWING

BUG JOURNAL

DATE:		TIME:		SEASON:	○ SPRING ○ SUMMER ○ FALL ○ WINTER

WEATHER CONDITIONS:	○ HOT ○ WARM ○ SUNNY ○ CLOUDY ○ RAINY ○ WINDY ○ FOGGY ○ COLD
BUG NAME:	
WHERE DID YOU FIND IT?	
WHAT COLOR(S) IS THE BUG?	

NUMBER OF LEGS?		DOES IT HAVE WINGS?	○ YES ○ NO ○ NOT SURE
NUMBER OF LEGS?			

THE BUG IS...	○ BIG ○ SHINY ○ FAST ○ SCARY ○ LITTLE ○ SLOW ○ CUTE ○ ROUND ○ THIN

DOES IT MAKE ANY SOUND?	○ YES ○ NO	WAS IT ALONE OR IN A GROUP?	○ ALONE ○ GROUP

NOTES

PHOTO/DRAWING

BUG JOURNAL

DATE:		TIME:		SEASON:	○ SPRING ○ SUMMER ○ FALL ○ WINTER

WEATHER CONDITIONS:	○ HOT ○ WARM ○ SUNNY ○ CLOUDY ○ RAINY ○ WINDY ○ FOGGY ○ COLD
BUG NAME:	
WHERE DID YOU FIND IT?	
WHAT COLOR(S) IS THE BUG?	

NUMBER OF LEGS?		DOES IT HAVE WINGS?	○ YES ○ NO ○ NOT SURE

NUMBER OF LEGS?	
THE BUG IS...	○ BIG ○ SHINY ○ FAST ○ SCARY ○ LITTLE ○ SLOW ○ CUTE ○ ROUND ○ THIN

DOES IT MAKE ANY SOUND?	○ YES ○ NO	WAS IT ALONE OR IN A GROUP?	○ ALONE ○ GROUP

NOTES

PHOTO/DRAWING

BUG JOURNAL

DATE:		TIME:		SEASON:	○ SPRING ○ SUMMER ○ FALL ○ WINTER

WEATHER CONDITIONS:	○ HOT ○ WARM ○ SUNNY ○ CLOUDY ○ RAINY ○ WINDY ○ FOGGY ○ COLD
BUG NAME:	
WHERE DID YOU FIND IT?	
WHAT COLOR(S) IS THE BUG?	

NUMBER OF LEGS?		DOES IT HAVE WINGS?	○ YES ○ NO ○ NOT SURE

NUMBER OF LEGS?	
THE BUG IS...	○ BIG ○ SHINY ○ FAST ○ SCARY ○ LITTLE ○ SLOW ○ CUTE ○ ROUND ○ THIN

DOES IT MAKE ANY SOUND?	○ YES ○ NO	WAS IT ALONE OR IN A GROUP?	○ ALONE ○ GROUP

NOTES

PHOTO/DRAWING

BUG JOURNAL

DATE:		TIME:		SEASON:	○ SPRING ○ SUMMER ○ FALL ○ WINTER

WEATHER CONDITIONS:	○ HOT ○ WARM ○ SUNNY ○ CLOUDY ○ RAINY ○ WINDY ○ FOGGY ○ COLD
BUG NAME:	
WHERE DID YOU FIND IT?	
WHAT COLOR(S) IS THE BUG?	

NUMBER OF LEGS?		DOES IT HAVE WINGS?	○ YES ○ NO ○ NOT SURE

NUMBER OF LEGS?	
THE BUG IS...	○ BIG ○ SHINY ○ FAST ○ SCARY ○ LITTLE ○ SLOW ○ CUTE ○ ROUND ○ THIN

DOES IT MAKE ANY SOUND?	○ YES ○ NO	WAS IT ALONE OR IN A GROUP?	○ ALONE ○ GROUP

NOTES

PHOTO/DRAWING

BUG JOURNAL

DATE:		TIME:		SEASON:	○ SPRING ○ SUMMER ○ FALL ○ WINTER

WEATHER CONDITIONS:	○ HOT ○ WARM ○ SUNNY ○ CLOUDY ○ RAINY ○ WINDY ○ FOGGY ○ COLD
BUG NAME:	
WHERE DID YOU FIND IT?	
WHAT COLOR(S) IS THE BUG?	

NUMBER OF LEGS?		DOES IT HAVE WINGS?	○ YES ○ NO ○ NOT SURE
NUMBER OF LEGS?			
THE BUG IS...	○ BIG ○ SHINY ○ FAST ○ SCARY ○ LITTLE ○ SLOW ○ CUTE ○ ROUND ○ THIN		
DOES IT MAKE ANY SOUND?	○ YES ○ NO	WAS IT ALONE OR IN A GROUP?	○ ALONE ○ GROUP

NOTES

PHOTO/DRAWING

BUG JOURNAL

DATE:		TIME:		SEASON:	○ SPRING ○ SUMMER ○ FALL ○ WINTER
WEATHER CONDITIONS:		○ HOT ○ WARM ○ SUNNY ○ CLOUDY ○ RAINY ○ WINDY ○ FOGGY ○ COLD			
BUG NAME:					
WHERE DID YOU FIND IT?					
WHAT COLOR(S) IS THE BUG?					
NUMBER OF LEGS?		DOES IT HAVE WINGS?	○ YES ○ NO ○ NOT SURE		
NUMBER OF LEGS?					
THE BUG IS...		○ BIG ○ SHINY ○ FAST ○ SCARY ○ LITTLE ○ SLOW ○ CUTE ○ ROUND ○ THIN			
DOES IT MAKE ANY SOUND?	○ YES ○ NO	WAS IT ALONE OR IN A GROUP?	○ ALONE ○ GROUP		

NOTES

PHOTO/DRAWING

BUG JOURNAL

DATE:		TIME:		SEASON:	○ SPRING ○ SUMMER ○ FALL ○ WINTER

WEATHER CONDITIONS:	○ HOT ○ WARM ○ SUNNY ○ CLOUDY ○ RAINY ○ WINDY ○ FOGGY ○ COLD
BUG NAME:	
WHERE DID YOU FIND IT?	
WHAT COLOR(S) IS THE BUG?	

NUMBER OF LEGS?		DOES IT HAVE WINGS?	○ YES ○ NO ○ NOT SURE

NUMBER OF LEGS?	
THE BUG IS...	○ BIG ○ SHINY ○ FAST ○ SCARY ○ LITTLE ○ SLOW ○ CUTE ○ ROUND ○ THIN

DOES IT MAKE ANY SOUND?	○ YES ○ NO	WAS IT ALONE OR IN A GROUP?	○ ALONE ○ GROUP

NOTES

PHOTO/DRAWING

BUG JOURNAL

DATE:		TIME:		SEASON:	○ SPRING ○ SUMMER ○ FALL ○ WINTER

WEATHER CONDITIONS:	○ HOT ○ WARM ○ SUNNY ○ CLOUDY ○ RAINY ○ WINDY ○ FOGGY ○ COLD
BUG NAME:	
WHERE DID YOU FIND IT?	
WHAT COLOR(S) IS THE BUG?	

NUMBER OF LEGS?		DOES IT HAVE WINGS?	○ YES ○ NO ○ NOT SURE
NUMBER OF LEGS?			

THE BUG IS...	○ BIG ○ SHINY ○ FAST ○ SCARY ○ LITTLE ○ SLOW ○ CUTE ○ ROUND ○ THIN

DOES IT MAKE ANY SOUND?	○ YES ○ NO	WAS IT ALONE OR IN A GROUP?	○ ALONE ○ GROUP

NOTES

PHOTO/DRAWING

BUG JOURNAL

DATE:		TIME:		SEASON:	○ SPRING ○ SUMMER ○ FALL ○ WINTER

WEATHER CONDITIONS:	○ HOT ○ WARM ○ SUNNY ○ CLOUDY ○ RAINY ○ WINDY ○ FOGGY ○ COLD
BUG NAME:	
WHERE DID YOU FIND IT?	
WHAT COLOR(S) IS THE BUG?	

NUMBER OF LEGS?		DOES IT HAVE WINGS?	○ YES ○ NO ○ NOT SURE
NUMBER OF LEGS?			

THE BUG IS...	○ BIG ○ SHINY ○ FAST ○ SCARY ○ LITTLE ○ SLOW ○ CUTE ○ ROUND ○ THIN

DOES IT MAKE ANY SOUND?	○ YES ○ NO	WAS IT ALONE OR IN A GROUP?	○ ALONE ○ GROUP

NOTES

PHOTO/DRAWING

BUG JOURNAL

DATE:		TIME:		SEASON:	○ SPRING ○ SUMMER ○ FALL ○ WINTER

WEATHER CONDITIONS:	○ HOT ○ WARM ○ SUNNY ○ CLOUDY ○ RAINY ○ WINDY ○ FOGGY ○ COLD
BUG NAME:	
WHERE DID YOU FIND IT?	
WHAT COLOR(S) IS THE BUG?	

NUMBER OF LEGS?		DOES IT HAVE WINGS?	○ YES ○ NO ○ NOT SURE

NUMBER OF LEGS?	
THE BUG IS...	○ BIG ○ SHINY ○ FAST ○ SCARY ○ LITTLE ○ SLOW ○ CUTE ○ ROUND ○ THIN

DOES IT MAKE ANY SOUND?	○ YES ○ NO	WAS IT ALONE OR IN A GROUP?	○ ALONE ○ GROUP

NOTES

PHOTO/DRAWING

BUG JOURNAL

DATE:		TIME:		SEASON:	○ SPRING ○ SUMMER ○ FALL ○ WINTER
WEATHER CONDITIONS:			○ HOT ○ WARM ○ SUNNY ○ CLOUDY ○ RAINY ○ WINDY ○ FOGGY ○ COLD		
BUG NAME:					
WHERE DID YOU FIND IT?					
WHAT COLOR(S) IS THE BUG?					
NUMBER OF LEGS?			**DOES IT HAVE WINGS?**	○ YES ○ NO ○ NOT SURE	
NUMBER OF LEGS?					
THE BUG IS...			○ BIG ○ SHINY ○ FAST ○ SCARY ○ LITTLE ○ SLOW ○ CUTE ○ ROUND ○ THIN		
DOES IT MAKE ANY SOUND?	○ YES ○ NO		**WAS IT ALONE OR IN A GROUP?**	○ ALONE ○ GROUP	

NOTES

PHOTO/DRAWING

BUG JOURNAL

DATE:		TIME:		SEASON:	○ SPRING ○ SUMMER ○ FALL ○ WINTER

WEATHER CONDITIONS:	○ HOT ○ WARM ○ SUNNY ○ CLOUDY ○ RAINY ○ WINDY ○ FOGGY ○ COLD
BUG NAME:	
WHERE DID YOU FIND IT?	
WHAT COLOR(S) IS THE BUG?	

NUMBER OF LEGS?		DOES IT HAVE WINGS?	○ YES ○ NO ○ NOT SURE

NUMBER OF LEGS?	
THE BUG IS...	○ BIG ○ SHINY ○ FAST ○ SCARY ○ LITTLE ○ SLOW ○ CUTE ○ ROUND ○ THIN

DOES IT MAKE ANY SOUND?	○ YES ○ NO	WAS IT ALONE OR IN A GROUP?	○ ALONE ○ GROUP

NOTES

PHOTO/DRAWING

BUG JOURNAL

DATE:		TIME:		SEASON:	○ SPRING ○ SUMMER ○ FALL ○ WINTER

WEATHER CONDITIONS:	○ HOT ○ WARM ○ SUNNY ○ CLOUDY ○ RAINY ○ WINDY ○ FOGGY ○ COLD
BUG NAME:	
WHERE DID YOU FIND IT?	
WHAT COLOR(S) IS THE BUG?	

NUMBER OF LEGS?		DOES IT HAVE WINGS?	○ YES ○ NO ○ NOT SURE

NUMBER OF LEGS?	
THE BUG IS...	○ BIG ○ SHINY ○ FAST ○ SCARY ○ LITTLE ○ SLOW ○ CUTE ○ ROUND ○ THIN

DOES IT MAKE ANY SOUND?	○ YES ○ NO	WAS IT ALONE OR IN A GROUP?	○ ALONE ○ GROUP

NOTES

PHOTO/DRAWING

BUG JOURNAL

DATE:			TIME:		SEASON:	○ SPRING ○ SUMMER ○ FALL ○ WINTER

WEATHER CONDITIONS:	○ HOT ○ WARM ○ SUNNY ○ CLOUDY ○ RAINY ○ WINDY ○ FOGGY ○ COLD
BUG NAME:	
WHERE DID YOU FIND IT?	
WHAT COLOR(S) IS THE BUG?	

NUMBER OF LEGS?		DOES IT HAVE WINGS?	○ YES ○ NO ○ NOT SURE

NUMBER OF LEGS?	
THE BUG IS...	○ BIG ○ SHINY ○ FAST ○ SCARY ○ LITTLE ○ SLOW ○ CUTE ○ ROUND ○ THIN

DOES IT MAKE ANY SOUND?	○ YES ○ NO	WAS IT ALONE OR IN A GROUP?	○ ALONE ○ GROUP

NOTES

PHOTO/DRAWING

BUG JOURNAL

DATE:		TIME:		SEASON:	○ SPRING ○ SUMMER ○ FALL ○ WINTER

WEATHER CONDITIONS:	○ HOT ○ WARM ○ SUNNY ○ CLOUDY ○ RAINY ○ WINDY ○ FOGGY ○ COLD
BUG NAME:	
WHERE DID YOU FIND IT?	
WHAT COLOR(S) IS THE BUG?	

NUMBER OF LEGS?		DOES IT HAVE WINGS?	○ YES ○ NO ○ NOT SURE

NUMBER OF LEGS?	
THE BUG IS...	○ BIG ○ SHINY ○ FAST ○ SCARY ○ LITTLE ○ SLOW ○ CUTE ○ ROUND ○ THIN

DOES IT MAKE ANY SOUND?	○ YES ○ NO	WAS IT ALONE OR IN A GROUP?	○ ALONE ○ GROUP

NOTES

PHOTO/DRAWING

BUG JOURNAL

DATE:		TIME:		SEASON:	○ SPRING ○ SUMMER ○ FALL ○ WINTER
WEATHER CONDITIONS:		○ HOT ○ WARM ○ SUNNY ○ CLOUDY ○ RAINY ○ WINDY ○ FOGGY ○ COLD			
BUG NAME:					
WHERE DID YOU FIND IT?					
WHAT COLOR(S) IS THE BUG?					
NUMBER OF LEGS?		**DOES IT HAVE WINGS?**	○ YES ○ NO ○ NOT SURE		
NUMBER OF LEGS?					
THE BUG IS...		○ BIG ○ SHINY ○ FAST ○ SCARY ○ LITTLE ○ SLOW ○ CUTE ○ ROUND ○ THIN			
DOES IT MAKE ANY SOUND?	○ YES ○ NO	**WAS IT ALONE OR IN A GROUP?**	○ ALONE ○ GROUP		

NOTES

PHOTO/DRAWING

BUG JOURNAL

DATE:		TIME:		SEASON:	○ SPRING ○ SUMMER ○ FALL ○ WINTER

WEATHER CONDITIONS:	○ HOT ○ WARM ○ SUNNY ○ CLOUDY ○ RAINY ○ WINDY ○ FOGGY ○ COLD
BUG NAME:	
WHERE DID YOU FIND IT?	
WHAT COLOR(S) IS THE BUG?	

NUMBER OF LEGS?		DOES IT HAVE WINGS?	○ YES ○ NO ○ NOT SURE
NUMBER OF LEGS?			
THE BUG IS...	○ BIG ○ SHINY ○ FAST ○ SCARY ○ LITTLE ○ SLOW ○ CUTE ○ ROUND ○ THIN		
DOES IT MAKE ANY SOUND?	○ YES ○ NO	WAS IT ALONE OR IN A GROUP?	○ ALONE ○ GROUP

NOTES

PHOTO/DRAWING

BUG JOURNAL

DATE:		TIME:		SEASON:	○ SPRING ○ SUMMER ○ FALL ○ WINTER
WEATHER CONDITIONS:			○ HOT ○ WARM ○ SUNNY ○ CLOUDY ○ RAINY ○ WINDY ○ FOGGY ○ COLD		
BUG NAME:						
WHERE DID YOU FIND IT?						
WHAT COLOR(S) IS THE BUG?						
NUMBER OF LEGS?			DOES IT HAVE WINGS?	○ YES ○ NO ○ NOT SURE	
NUMBER OF LEGS?						
THE BUG IS...			○ BIG ○ SHINY ○ FAST ○ SCARY ○ LITTLE ○ SLOW ○ CUTE ○ ROUND ○ THIN		
DOES IT MAKE ANY SOUND?	○ YES ○ NO		WAS IT ALONE OR IN A GROUP?	○ ALONE ○ GROUP	

NOTES

PHOTO/DRAWING

BUG JOURNAL

DATE:		TIME:		SEASON:	○ SPRING ○ SUMMER ○ FALL ○ WINTER
WEATHER CONDITIONS:		○ HOT ○ WARM ○ SUNNY ○ CLOUDY ○ RAINY ○ WINDY ○ FOGGY ○ COLD			
BUG NAME:					
WHERE DID YOU FIND IT?					
WHAT COLOR(S) IS THE BUG?					
NUMBER OF LEGS?		DOES IT HAVE WINGS?	○ YES ○ NO ○ NOT SURE		
NUMBER OF LEGS?					
THE BUG IS...		○ BIG ○ SHINY ○ FAST ○ SCARY ○ LITTLE ○ SLOW ○ CUTE ○ ROUND ○ THIN			
DOES IT MAKE ANY SOUND?	○ YES ○ NO	WAS IT ALONE OR IN A GROUP?	○ ALONE ○ GROUP		

NOTES

PHOTO/DRAWING

BUG JOURNAL

DATE:		TIME:		SEASON:	○ SPRING ○ SUMMER ○ FALL ○ WINTER
WEATHER CONDITIONS:		○ HOT ○ WARM ○ SUNNY ○ CLOUDY ○ RAINY ○ WINDY ○ FOGGY ○ COLD			
BUG NAME:					
WHERE DID YOU FIND IT?					
WHAT COLOR(S) IS THE BUG?					
NUMBER OF LEGS?		**DOES IT HAVE WINGS?**	○ YES ○ NO ○ NOT SURE		
NUMBER OF LEGS?					
THE BUG IS...		○ BIG ○ SHINY ○ FAST ○ SCARY ○ LITTLE ○ SLOW ○ CUTE ○ ROUND ○ THIN			
DOES IT MAKE ANY SOUND?	○ YES ○ NO	**WAS IT ALONE OR IN A GROUP?**	○ ALONE ○ GROUP		

NOTES

PHOTO/DRAWING

BUG JOURNAL

DATE:		TIME:		SEASON:	○ SPRING ○ SUMMER ○ FALL ○ WINTER
WEATHER CONDITIONS:		○ HOT ○ WARM ○ SUNNY ○ CLOUDY ○ RAINY ○ WINDY ○ FOGGY ○ COLD			
BUG NAME:					
WHERE DID YOU FIND IT?					
WHAT COLOR(S) IS THE BUG?					
NUMBER OF LEGS?		**DOES IT HAVE WINGS?**	○ YES ○ NO ○ NOT SURE		
NUMBER OF LEGS?					
THE BUG IS...		○ BIG ○ SHINY ○ FAST ○ SCARY ○ LITTLE ○ SLOW ○ CUTE ○ ROUND ○ THIN			
DOES IT MAKE ANY SOUND?	○ YES ○ NO	**WAS IT ALONE OR IN A GROUP?**		○ ALONE ○ GROUP	

NOTES

PHOTO/DRAWING

BUG JOURNAL

DATE:		TIME:		SEASON:	○ SPRING ○ SUMMER ○ FALL ○ WINTER
WEATHER CONDITIONS:		○ HOT ○ WARM ○ SUNNY ○ CLOUDY ○ RAINY ○ WINDY ○ FOGGY ○ COLD			
BUG NAME:					
WHERE DID YOU FIND IT?					
WHAT COLOR(S) IS THE BUG?					
NUMBER OF LEGS?		**DOES IT HAVE WINGS?**	○ YES ○ NO ○ NOT SURE		
NUMBER OF LEGS?					
THE BUG IS...		○ BIG ○ SHINY ○ FAST ○ SCARY ○ LITTLE ○ SLOW ○ CUTE ○ ROUND ○ THIN			
DOES IT MAKE ANY SOUND?	○ YES ○ NO	**WAS IT ALONE OR IN A GROUP?**	○ ALONE ○ GROUP		

NOTES

PHOTO/DRAWING

BUG JOURNAL

DATE:		TIME:		SEASON:	○ SPRING ○ SUMMER ○ FALL ○ WINTER

WEATHER CONDITIONS:	○ HOT ○ WARM ○ SUNNY ○ CLOUDY ○ RAINY ○ WINDY ○ FOGGY ○ COLD
BUG NAME:	
WHERE DID YOU FIND IT?	
WHAT COLOR(S) IS THE BUG?	

NUMBER OF LEGS?		DOES IT HAVE WINGS?	○ YES ○ NO ○ NOT SURE

NUMBER OF LEGS?	
THE BUG IS...	○ BIG ○ SHINY ○ FAST ○ SCARY ○ LITTLE ○ SLOW ○ CUTE ○ ROUND ○ THIN

DOES IT MAKE ANY SOUND?	○ YES ○ NO	WAS IT ALONE OR IN A GROUP?	○ ALONE ○ GROUP

NOTES

PHOTO/DRAWING

BUG JOURNAL

DATE:		TIME:		SEASON:	○ SPRING ○ SUMMER ○ FALL ○ WINTER
WEATHER CONDITIONS:		○ HOT ○ WARM ○ SUNNY ○ CLOUDY ○ RAINY ○ WINDY ○ FOGGY ○ COLD			
BUG NAME:					
WHERE DID YOU FIND IT?					
WHAT COLOR(S) IS THE BUG?					
NUMBER OF LEGS?			**DOES IT HAVE WINGS?**	○ YES ○ NO ○ NOT SURE	
NUMBER OF LEGS?					
THE BUG IS...		○ BIG ○ SHINY ○ FAST ○ SCARY ○ LITTLE ○ SLOW ○ CUTE ○ ROUND ○ THIN			
DOES IT MAKE ANY SOUND?	○ YES ○ NO	**WAS IT ALONE OR IN A GROUP?**		○ ALONE ○ GROUP	

NOTES

PHOTO/DRAWING

BUG JOURNAL

DATE:		TIME:		SEASON:	○ SPRING ○ SUMMER ○ FALL ○ WINTER

WEATHER CONDITIONS:	○ HOT ○ WARM ○ SUNNY ○ CLOUDY ○ RAINY ○ WINDY ○ FOGGY ○ COLD
BUG NAME:	
WHERE DID YOU FIND IT?	
WHAT COLOR(S) IS THE BUG?	

NUMBER OF LEGS?		DOES IT HAVE WINGS?	○ YES ○ NO ○ NOT SURE
NUMBER OF LEGS?			
THE BUG IS...	○ BIG ○ SHINY ○ FAST ○ SCARY ○ LITTLE ○ SLOW ○ CUTE ○ ROUND ○ THIN		
DOES IT MAKE ANY SOUND?	○ YES ○ NO	WAS IT ALONE OR IN A GROUP?	○ ALONE ○ GROUP

NOTES

PHOTO/DRAWING

BUG JOURNAL

DATE:		TIME:		SEASON:	○ SPRING ○ SUMMER ○ FALL ○ WINTER
WEATHER CONDITIONS:				○ HOT ○ WARM ○ SUNNY ○ CLOUDY ○ RAINY ○ WINDY ○ FOGGY ○ COLD	
BUG NAME:					
WHERE DID YOU FIND IT?					
WHAT COLOR(S) IS THE BUG?					
NUMBER OF LEGS?			DOES IT HAVE WINGS?	○ YES ○ NO ○ NOT SURE	
NUMBER OF LEGS?					
THE BUG IS...		○ BIG ○ SHINY ○ FAST ○ SCARY ○ LITTLE ○ SLOW ○ CUTE ○ ROUND ○ THIN			
DOES IT MAKE ANY SOUND?	○ YES ○ NO	WAS IT ALONE OR IN A GROUP?		○ ALONE ○ GROUP	

NOTES

PHOTO/DRAWING

BUG JOURNAL

DATE:		TIME:		SEASON:	○ SPRING ○ SUMMER ○ FALL ○ WINTER

WEATHER CONDITIONS:	○ HOT ○ WARM ○ SUNNY ○ CLOUDY ○ RAINY ○ WINDY ○ FOGGY ○ COLD
BUG NAME:	
WHERE DID YOU FIND IT?	
WHAT COLOR(S) IS THE BUG?	

NUMBER OF LEGS?		DOES IT HAVE WINGS?	○ YES ○ NO ○ NOT SURE

NUMBER OF LEGS?	
THE BUG IS...	○ BIG ○ SHINY ○ FAST ○ SCARY ○ LITTLE ○ SLOW ○ CUTE ○ ROUND ○ THIN

DOES IT MAKE ANY SOUND?	○ YES ○ NO	WAS IT ALONE OR IN A GROUP?	○ ALONE ○ GROUP

NOTES

PHOTO/DRAWING

BUG JOURNAL

DATE:		TIME:		SEASON:	○ SPRING ○ SUMMER ○ FALL ○ WINTER

WEATHER CONDITIONS:	○ HOT ○ WARM ○ SUNNY ○ CLOUDY ○ RAINY ○ WINDY ○ FOGGY ○ COLD
BUG NAME:	
WHERE DID YOU FIND IT?	
WHAT COLOR(S) IS THE BUG?	

NUMBER OF LEGS?		DOES IT HAVE WINGS?	○ YES ○ NO ○ NOT SURE

NUMBER OF LEGS?	
THE BUG IS...	○ BIG ○ SHINY ○ FAST ○ SCARY ○ LITTLE ○ SLOW ○ CUTE ○ ROUND ○ THIN

DOES IT MAKE ANY SOUND?	○ YES ○ NO	WAS IT ALONE OR IN A GROUP?	○ ALONE ○ GROUP

NOTES

PHOTO/DRAWING

BUG JOURNAL

DATE:		TIME:		SEASON:	○ SPRING ○ SUMMER ○ FALL ○ WINTER

WEATHER CONDITIONS:	○ HOT ○ WARM ○ SUNNY ○ CLOUDY ○ RAINY ○ WINDY ○ FOGGY ○ COLD
BUG NAME:	
WHERE DID YOU FIND IT?	
WHAT COLOR(S) IS THE BUG?	

NUMBER OF LEGS?		DOES IT HAVE WINGS?	○ YES ○ NO ○ NOT SURE

NUMBER OF LEGS?	
THE BUG IS...	○ BIG ○ SHINY ○ FAST ○ SCARY ○ LITTLE ○ SLOW ○ CUTE ○ ROUND ○ THIN

DOES IT MAKE ANY SOUND?	○ YES ○ NO	WAS IT ALONE OR IN A GROUP?	○ ALONE ○ GROUP

NOTES

PHOTO/DRAWING

BUG JOURNAL

DATE:		TIME:		SEASON:	○ SPRING ○ SUMMER ○ FALL ○ WINTER
WEATHER CONDITIONS:		○ HOT ○ WARM ○ SUNNY ○ CLOUDY ○ RAINY ○ WINDY ○ FOGGY ○ COLD			
BUG NAME:					
WHERE DID YOU FIND IT?					
WHAT COLOR(S) IS THE BUG?					
NUMBER OF LEGS?		DOES IT HAVE WINGS?		○ YES ○ NO ○ NOT SURE	
NUMBER OF LEGS?					
THE BUG IS...		○ BIG ○ SHINY ○ FAST ○ SCARY ○ LITTLE ○ SLOW ○ CUTE ○ ROUND ○ THIN			
DOES IT MAKE ANY SOUND?	○ YES ○ NO	WAS IT ALONE OR IN A GROUP?		○ ALONE ○ GROUP	

NOTES

PHOTO/DRAWING

BUG JOURNAL

DATE:		TIME:		SEASON:	○ SPRING ○ SUMMER ○ FALL ○ WINTER

WEATHER CONDITIONS:	○ HOT ○ WARM ○ SUNNY ○ CLOUDY ○ RAINY ○ WINDY ○ FOGGY ○ COLD
BUG NAME:	
WHERE DID YOU FIND IT?	
WHAT COLOR(S) IS THE BUG?	

NUMBER OF LEGS?		DOES IT HAVE WINGS?	○ YES ○ NO ○ NOT SURE

NUMBER OF LEGS?	
THE BUG IS...	○ BIG ○ SHINY ○ FAST ○ SCARY ○ LITTLE ○ SLOW ○ CUTE ○ ROUND ○ THIN

DOES IT MAKE ANY SOUND?	○ YES ○ NO	WAS IT ALONE OR IN A GROUP?	○ ALONE ○ GROUP

NOTES

PHOTO/DRAWING

BUG JOURNAL

DATE:		TIME:		SEASON:	○ SPRING ○ SUMMER ○ FALL ○ WINTER

WEATHER CONDITIONS:	○ HOT ○ WARM ○ SUNNY ○ CLOUDY ○ RAINY ○ WINDY ○ FOGGY ○ COLD
BUG NAME:	
WHERE DID YOU FIND IT?	
WHAT COLOR(S) IS THE BUG?	

NUMBER OF LEGS?		DOES IT HAVE WINGS?	○ YES ○ NO ○ NOT SURE

NUMBER OF LEGS?	
THE BUG IS…	○ BIG ○ SHINY ○ FAST ○ SCARY ○ LITTLE ○ SLOW ○ CUTE ○ ROUND ○ THIN

DOES IT MAKE ANY SOUND?	○ YES ○ NO	WAS IT ALONE OR IN A GROUP?	○ ALONE ○ GROUP

NOTES

PHOTO/DRAWING

BUG JOURNAL

DATE:		TIME:		SEASON:	○ SPRING ○ SUMMER ○ FALL ○ WINTER

WEATHER CONDITIONS:	○ HOT ○ WARM ○ SUNNY ○ CLOUDY ○ RAINY ○ WINDY ○ FOGGY ○ COLD
BUG NAME:	
WHERE DID YOU FIND IT?	
WHAT COLOR(S) IS THE BUG?	

NUMBER OF LEGS?		DOES IT HAVE WINGS?	○ YES ○ NO ○ NOT SURE

NUMBER OF LEGS?	
THE BUG IS...	○ BIG ○ SHINY ○ FAST ○ SCARY ○ LITTLE ○ SLOW ○ CUTE ○ ROUND ○ THIN

DOES IT MAKE ANY SOUND?	○ YES ○ NO	WAS IT ALONE OR IN A GROUP?	○ ALONE ○ GROUP

NOTES

PHOTO/DRAWING

BUG JOURNAL

DATE:		TIME:		SEASON:	○ SPRING ○ SUMMER ○ FALL ○ WINTER
WEATHER CONDITIONS:		○ HOT ○ WARM ○ SUNNY ○ CLOUDY ○ RAINY ○ WINDY ○ FOGGY ○ COLD			
BUG NAME:					
WHERE DID YOU FIND IT?					
WHAT COLOR(S) IS THE BUG?					
NUMBER OF LEGS?		DOES IT HAVE WINGS?	○ YES ○ NO ○ NOT SURE		
NUMBER OF LEGS?					
THE BUG IS...		○ BIG ○ SHINY ○ FAST ○ SCARY ○ LITTLE ○ SLOW ○ CUTE ○ ROUND ○ THIN			
DOES IT MAKE ANY SOUND?	○ YES ○ NO	WAS IT ALONE OR IN A GROUP?	○ ALONE ○ GROUP		

NOTES

PHOTO/DRAWING

BUG JOURNAL

DATE:		TIME:		SEASON:	○ SPRING ○ SUMMER ○ FALL ○ WINTER

WEATHER CONDITIONS:	○ HOT ○ WARM ○ SUNNY ○ CLOUDY ○ RAINY ○ WINDY ○ FOGGY ○ COLD
BUG NAME:	
WHERE DID YOU FIND IT?	
WHAT COLOR(S) IS THE BUG?	

NUMBER OF LEGS?		DOES IT HAVE WINGS?	○ YES ○ NO ○ NOT SURE

NUMBER OF LEGS?	
THE BUG IS...	○ BIG ○ SHINY ○ FAST ○ SCARY ○ LITTLE ○ SLOW ○ CUTE ○ ROUND ○ THIN

DOES IT MAKE ANY SOUND?	○ YES ○ NO	WAS IT ALONE OR IN A GROUP?	○ ALONE ○ GROUP

NOTES

PHOTO/DRAWING

BUG JOURNAL

DATE:		TIME:		SEASON:	○ SPRING ○ SUMMER ○ FALL ○ WINTER
WEATHER CONDITIONS:		○ HOT ○ WARM ○ SUNNY ○ CLOUDY ○ RAINY ○ WINDY ○ FOGGY ○ COLD			
BUG NAME:					
WHERE DID YOU FIND IT?					
WHAT COLOR(S) IS THE BUG?					
NUMBER OF LEGS?		**DOES IT HAVE WINGS?**	○ YES ○ NO ○ NOT SURE		
NUMBER OF LEGS?					
THE BUG IS...		○ BIG ○ SHINY ○ FAST ○ SCARY ○ LITTLE ○ SLOW ○ CUTE ○ ROUND ○ THIN			
DOES IT MAKE ANY SOUND?	○ YES ○ NO	**WAS IT ALONE OR IN A GROUP?**		○ ALONE ○ GROUP	

NOTES

PHOTO/DRAWING

BUG JOURNAL

DATE:		TIME:		SEASON:	○ SPRING ○ SUMMER ○ FALL ○ WINTER

WEATHER CONDITIONS:	○ HOT ○ WARM ○ SUNNY ○ CLOUDY ○ RAINY ○ WINDY ○ FOGGY ○ COLD
BUG NAME:	
WHERE DID YOU FIND IT?	
WHAT COLOR(S) IS THE BUG?	

NUMBER OF LEGS?		DOES IT HAVE WINGS?	○ YES ○ NO ○ NOT SURE

NUMBER OF LEGS?	
THE BUG IS...	○ BIG ○ SHINY ○ FAST ○ SCARY ○ LITTLE ○ SLOW ○ CUTE ○ ROUND ○ THIN

DOES IT MAKE ANY SOUND?	○ YES ○ NO	WAS IT ALONE OR IN A GROUP?	○ ALONE ○ GROUP

NOTES

PHOTO/DRAWING

BUG JOURNAL

DATE:		TIME:		SEASON:	○ SPRING ○ SUMMER ○ FALL ○ WINTER

WEATHER CONDITIONS:	○ HOT ○ WARM ○ SUNNY ○ CLOUDY ○ RAINY ○ WINDY ○ FOGGY ○ COLD
BUG NAME:	
WHERE DID YOU FIND IT?	
WHAT COLOR(S) IS THE BUG?	

NUMBER OF LEGS?		DOES IT HAVE WINGS?	○ YES ○ NO ○ NOT SURE

NUMBER OF LEGS?	
THE BUG IS...	○ BIG ○ SHINY ○ FAST ○ SCARY ○ LITTLE ○ SLOW ○ CUTE ○ ROUND ○ THIN

DOES IT MAKE ANY SOUND?	○ YES ○ NO	WAS IT ALONE OR IN A GROUP?	○ ALONE ○ GROUP

NOTES

PHOTO/DRAWING

BUG JOURNAL

DATE:		TIME:		SEASON:	○ SPRING ○ SUMMER ○ FALL ○ WINTER

WEATHER CONDITIONS:	○ HOT ○ WARM ○ SUNNY ○ CLOUDY ○ RAINY ○ WINDY ○ FOGGY ○ COLD
BUG NAME:	
WHERE DID YOU FIND IT?	
WHAT COLOR(S) IS THE BUG?	

NUMBER OF LEGS?		DOES IT HAVE WINGS?	○ YES ○ NO ○ NOT SURE

NUMBER OF LEGS?	
THE BUG IS...	○ BIG ○ SHINY ○ FAST ○ SCARY ○ LITTLE ○ SLOW ○ CUTE ○ ROUND ○ THIN

DOES IT MAKE ANY SOUND?	○ YES ○ NO	WAS IT ALONE OR IN A GROUP?	○ ALONE ○ GROUP

NOTES

PHOTO/DRAWING

BUG JOURNAL

DATE:		TIME:		SEASON:	○ SPRING ○ SUMMER ○ FALL ○ WINTER

WEATHER CONDITIONS:	○ HOT ○ WARM ○ SUNNY ○ CLOUDY ○ RAINY ○ WINDY ○ FOGGY ○ COLD
BUG NAME:	
WHERE DID YOU FIND IT?	
WHAT COLOR(S) IS THE BUG?	

NUMBER OF LEGS?		DOES IT HAVE WINGS?	○ YES ○ NO ○ NOT SURE

NUMBER OF LEGS?	
THE BUG IS...	○ BIG ○ SHINY ○ FAST ○ SCARY ○ LITTLE ○ SLOW ○ CUTE ○ ROUND ○ THIN

DOES IT MAKE ANY SOUND?	○ YES ○ NO	WAS IT ALONE OR IN A GROUP?	○ ALONE ○ GROUP

NOTES

PHOTO/DRAWING

BUG JOURNAL

DATE:		TIME:		SEASON:	○ SPRING ○ SUMMER ○ FALL ○ WINTER

WEATHER CONDITIONS:	○ HOT ○ WARM ○ SUNNY ○ CLOUDY ○ RAINY ○ WINDY ○ FOGGY ○ COLD
BUG NAME:	
WHERE DID YOU FIND IT?	
WHAT COLOR(S) IS THE BUG?	

NUMBER OF LEGS?		DOES IT HAVE WINGS?	○ YES ○ NO ○ NOT SURE

NUMBER OF LEGS?	
THE BUG IS...	○ BIG ○ SHINY ○ FAST ○ SCARY ○ LITTLE ○ SLOW ○ CUTE ○ ROUND ○ THIN

DOES IT MAKE ANY SOUND?	○ YES ○ NO	WAS IT ALONE OR IN A GROUP?	○ ALONE ○ GROUP

NOTES

PHOTO/DRAWING

BUG JOURNAL

DATE:		TIME:		SEASON:	○ SPRING ○ SUMMER ○ FALL ○ WINTER

WEATHER CONDITIONS:	○ HOT ○ WARM ○ SUNNY ○ CLOUDY ○ RAINY ○ WINDY ○ FOGGY ○ COLD
BUG NAME:	
WHERE DID YOU FIND IT?	
WHAT COLOR(S) IS THE BUG?	

NUMBER OF LEGS?		DOES IT HAVE WINGS?	○ YES ○ NO ○ NOT SURE

NUMBER OF LEGS?	
THE BUG IS...	○ BIG ○ SHINY ○ FAST ○ SCARY ○ LITTLE ○ SLOW ○ CUTE ○ ROUND ○ THIN

DOES IT MAKE ANY SOUND?	○ YES ○ NO	WAS IT ALONE OR IN A GROUP?	○ ALONE ○ GROUP

NOTES

PHOTO/DRAWING

BUG JOURNAL

DATE:		TIME:		SEASON:	○ SPRING ○ SUMMER ○ FALL ○ WINTER

WEATHER CONDITIONS:	○ HOT ○ WARM ○ SUNNY ○ CLOUDY ○ RAINY ○ WINDY ○ FOGGY ○ COLD

BUG NAME:	
WHERE DID YOU FIND IT?	
WHAT COLOR(S) IS THE BUG?	

NUMBER OF LEGS?		DOES IT HAVE WINGS?	○ YES ○ NO ○ NOT SURE

NUMBER OF LEGS?	

THE BUG IS...	○ BIG ○ SHINY ○ FAST ○ SCARY ○ LITTLE ○ SLOW ○ CUTE ○ ROUND ○ THIN

DOES IT MAKE ANY SOUND?	○ YES ○ NO	WAS IT ALONE OR IN A GROUP?	○ ALONE ○ GROUP

NOTES

PHOTO/DRAWING

BUG JOURNAL

DATE:		TIME:		SEASON:	○ SPRING ○ SUMMER ○ FALL ○ WINTER
WEATHER CONDITIONS:		○ HOT ○ WARM ○ SUNNY ○ CLOUDY ○ RAINY ○ WINDY ○ FOGGY ○ COLD			
BUG NAME:					
WHERE DID YOU FIND IT?					
WHAT COLOR(S) IS THE BUG?					
NUMBER OF LEGS?		**DOES IT HAVE WINGS?**	○ YES ○ NO ○ NOT SURE		
NUMBER OF LEGS?					
THE BUG IS...		○ BIG ○ SHINY ○ FAST ○ SCARY ○ LITTLE ○ SLOW ○ CUTE ○ ROUND ○ THIN			
DOES IT MAKE ANY SOUND?	○ YES ○ NO	**WAS IT ALONE OR IN A GROUP?**	○ ALONE ○ GROUP		

NOTES

PHOTO/DRAWING

BUG JOURNAL

DATE:		TIME:		SEASON:	○ SPRING ○ SUMMER ○ FALL ○ WINTER

WEATHER CONDITIONS:	○ HOT ○ WARM ○ SUNNY ○ CLOUDY ○ RAINY ○ WINDY ○ FOGGY ○ COLD
BUG NAME:	
WHERE DID YOU FIND IT?	
WHAT COLOR(S) IS THE BUG?	

NUMBER OF LEGS?		DOES IT HAVE WINGS?	○ YES ○ NO ○ NOT SURE

NUMBER OF LEGS?	
THE BUG IS...	○ BIG ○ SHINY ○ FAST ○ SCARY ○ LITTLE ○ SLOW ○ CUTE ○ ROUND ○ THIN

DOES IT MAKE ANY SOUND?	○ YES ○ NO	WAS IT ALONE OR IN A GROUP?	○ ALONE ○ GROUP

NOTES

PHOTO/DRAWING

BUG JOURNAL

DATE:		TIME:		SEASON:	○ SPRING ○ SUMMER ○ FALL ○ WINTER

WEATHER CONDITIONS:	○ HOT ○ WARM ○ SUNNY ○ CLOUDY ○ RAINY ○ WINDY ○ FOGGY ○ COLD
BUG NAME:	
WHERE DID YOU FIND IT?	
WHAT COLOR(S) IS THE BUG?	

NUMBER OF LEGS?		DOES IT HAVE WINGS?	○ YES ○ NO ○ NOT SURE

NUMBER OF LEGS?	
THE BUG IS...	○ BIG ○ SHINY ○ FAST ○ SCARY ○ LITTLE ○ SLOW ○ CUTE ○ ROUND ○ THIN

DOES IT MAKE ANY SOUND?	○ YES ○ NO	WAS IT ALONE OR IN A GROUP?	○ ALONE ○ GROUP

NOTES

PHOTO/DRAWING

BUG JOURNAL

DATE:		TIME:		SEASON:	○ SPRING ○ SUMMER ○ FALL ○ WINTER

WEATHER CONDITIONS:	○ HOT ○ WARM ○ SUNNY ○ CLOUDY ○ RAINY ○ WINDY ○ FOGGY ○ COLD
BUG NAME:	
WHERE DID YOU FIND IT?	
WHAT COLOR(S) IS THE BUG?	

NUMBER OF LEGS?		DOES IT HAVE WINGS?	○ YES ○ NO ○ NOT SURE

NUMBER OF LEGS?	
THE BUG IS...	○ BIG ○ SHINY ○ FAST ○ SCARY ○ LITTLE ○ SLOW ○ CUTE ○ ROUND ○ THIN

DOES IT MAKE ANY SOUND?	○ YES ○ NO	WAS IT ALONE OR IN A GROUP?	○ ALONE ○ GROUP

NOTES

PHOTO/DRAWING

BUG JOURNAL

DATE:		TIME:		SEASON:	○ SPRING ○ SUMMER ○ FALL ○ WINTER
WEATHER CONDITIONS:		○ HOT ○ WARM ○ SUNNY ○ CLOUDY ○ RAINY ○ WINDY ○ FOGGY ○ COLD			
BUG NAME:					
WHERE DID YOU FIND IT?					
WHAT COLOR(S) IS THE BUG?					
NUMBER OF LEGS?		**DOES IT HAVE WINGS?**	○ YES ○ NO ○ NOT SURE		
NUMBER OF LEGS?					
THE BUG IS...		○ BIG ○ SHINY ○ FAST ○ SCARY ○ LITTLE ○ SLOW ○ CUTE ○ ROUND ○ THIN			
DOES IT MAKE ANY SOUND?	○ YES ○ NO	**WAS IT ALONE OR IN A GROUP?**	○ ALONE ○ GROUP		

NOTES

PHOTO/DRAWING

BUG JOURNAL

DATE:		TIME:		SEASON:	○ SPRING ○ SUMMER ○ FALL ○ WINTER

WEATHER CONDITIONS:	○ HOT ○ WARM ○ SUNNY ○ CLOUDY ○ RAINY ○ WINDY ○ FOGGY ○ COLD
BUG NAME:	
WHERE DID YOU FIND IT?	
WHAT COLOR(S) IS THE BUG?	

NUMBER OF LEGS?		DOES IT HAVE WINGS?	○ YES ○ NO ○ NOT SURE
NUMBER OF LEGS?			

THE BUG IS...	○ BIG ○ SHINY ○ FAST ○ SCARY ○ LITTLE ○ SLOW ○ CUTE ○ ROUND ○ THIN

DOES IT MAKE ANY SOUND?	○ YES ○ NO	WAS IT ALONE OR IN A GROUP?	○ ALONE ○ GROUP

NOTES

PHOTO/DRAWING

BUG JOURNAL

DATE:			TIME:		SEASON:	○ SPRING ○ SUMMER ○ FALL ○ WINTER

WEATHER CONDITIONS:	○ HOT ○ WARM ○ SUNNY ○ CLOUDY ○ RAINY ○ WINDY ○ FOGGY ○ COLD
BUG NAME:	
WHERE DID YOU FIND IT?	
WHAT COLOR(S) IS THE BUG?	

NUMBER OF LEGS?		DOES IT HAVE WINGS?	○ YES ○ NO ○ NOT SURE

NUMBER OF LEGS?	
THE BUG IS...	○ BIG ○ SHINY ○ FAST ○ SCARY ○ LITTLE ○ SLOW ○ CUTE ○ ROUND ○ THIN

DOES IT MAKE ANY SOUND?	○ YES ○ NO	WAS IT ALONE OR IN A GROUP?	○ ALONE ○ GROUP

NOTES

PHOTO/DRAWING

www.ingramcontent.com/pod-product-compliance
Lightning Source LLC
Chambersburg PA
CBHW081148020426
42333CB00021B/2698